WHY WE MAKE GARDENS

(& OTHER POEMS)

for Marilyn Engle

keep making things grow —

Jeanne

WHY WE MAKE GARDENS

(& OTHER POEMS)

Jeanne Larsen

~~JEANNE LARSEN~~

MAYAPPLE PRESS 2010

Published by   MAYAPPLE PRESS
                 408 N. Lincoln St.
                 Bay City, MI 48708
                 www.mayapplepress.com

ISBN 978-0932412-95-9

ACKNOWLEDGMENTS

A number of these poems, some under variant titles, have appeared in *Appalachian Heritage*, *Blackbird*, *Center*, *Cimarron Review*, *The Cincinnati Review*, *Common Ground Review*, *The Eleventh Muse*, *The Florida Review*, *Folio*, *The Georgia Review*, *Green Mountains Review*, *The Literary Review*, *New Delta Review*, *Pleiades*, *Poetry East*, *Sewanee Review*, *So to Speak*, *Southern Poetry Review*, *Subtropics*, and *The Southern Poetry Anthology, Volume III: Southern Appalachia* (Texas Review Press). "The Garden of Languages" and "The Gazing-Globe Garden" also appeared on the Verse Daily website.

Versions of twenty-nine of the poems appeared with drawings by Jan Knipe in a privately-printed hand-bound art book entitled *These Gardens*, an edition of thirty copies. Particular thanks to Jan for permission to reproduce one of those fine drawings on the cover of this book.

Hearty thanks to Judith Kerman, as well as Amee Schmidt and Matthew Falk, without whom, no book. Or a clunker.

I'm also grateful to Tom Mesner, the Virginia Center for the Creative Arts, the Byrdcliffe Colony, the Ragdale Foundation, Hollins University, and the Cabell Faculty Fellowship fund for the gifts of time and space in which to make these poems.

Cover art "Kroger's Chrysanthemums" courtesy of Jan Knipe. Cover designed by Judith Kerman. Book designed and typest by Amee Schmidt with text in Bell MT, cover titles in Edda and poem titles in Belwe Lt BT. Author photo courtesy of R.H.W. Dillard.

Contents

(ANNIHILATING ALL THAT'S MADE)

(PLEASANCE)

Dear Marilyn,
I hope you find much
pleasure and "food
for thought" as you
leaf through these
verses of gardens!
Much happiness
in 2014.
Fondly,
Anne &
Tyson

The figure of this world I can compare,
To Garden plots and suchlike pleasaunt places.

—George Gascogine

The horns on the head of a rabbit are imagined but do not exist....
The form of the sun, moon, and stars are seen reflected in a
clear vessel of water.

—Hymn to the Dharmadhātu
(Donald S. Lopez, translator)

for Jan Knipe

with gratitude
for her friendship & her art

(ELEMENTALS)

THE GAZING-GLOBE GARDEN

is the element ether, a stuff
insubstantial as any that transits:

Carrara of columns, remembrance's
granite, acute

angles of mountains, the blunt
edge of a world.

Nonsense. It's
glass. It's merely

a mirror, a round-up
of jonquil, columbine, dwarf crested iris,

bellflowers' slow first sprigs.
It glistens, accepts,

sinks as the plants rise
toward their doubles.

It is what surrounds
it. Or it is

self-containing. Or
both, like the tangible bloom

of a face on its skin.

The Garden of Roses

against knowledge, defies
what runs down,

what lingers to eat at its watery
carbons. What it holds

was called *Purity, Agony, Timelessness,
Time.* Its blooms have been named

& been named *Beyond
naming,* flowering icons no one

can read. This much
at least—it blares *Beauty,* this garden

of shears, cruel trowels, light
poisons. A giver of wired, forced

festoons: it's loved for one thing.
Not its slackening.

Its captive, firm,
inarticulate thorns.

Midwinter Gardens

On a shelf, paperwhites swoon. Hot
house tulips sheared,

sheathed in a glass vase, spread

sepals wide. These flatten as stems droop.
They are tulips no more. One late
amaryllis, placed in the window, coolly

refuses to sprout. Outdoors

in snowfields, wrapped
by night's freezing rain, dried sedums'
lace-caps stand brown under polar

arisings: the passion of making,
the passion of being

unmade. All signal
resistance, stasis. All speak
of year's pivot, its pace, & the willed

twofold life of the borderland where,
for now, they exist.

GARDEN OF AIR

Sometimes it's syrup, some-

times, crinkled cellophane, whitewater
riffles. It's always the shapes:

around artemisia's stars, buddleia
spears, a soft fall

of cilantro. Shapes
around shape. It's evergreen ice

glancing off winter's ginger. Days,
mockingbirds harrow it, each

gash a contour line. Without
them, no map. Nights, it is turned

by the luna moth's flat, worked-jade
blade—& it breathes.

THE GARDEN OF WOOD

Is not built
of thick trunks & board-feet.

It yields. Or fractures.
It's a cavern of shadow,

luminous brown, chestnut
or oak, mahogany

red. It rots
into itself. Can be made

orderly. Yet prefers its own
stories: canopy, under

layer, roots coiled like fiddleheads.
It tends other gardens

with shreds of its skin.
Its secret is bending, is also

refusal to bend.

Hearing a Garden

Like a lyre, it
    curves. When Orpheus played,
        more than the trees danced: blood-
    grasses shimmied, cyclamens
tore themselves loose, rhythms

        of crocuses turned to the sun. Now
    it heaps up, crumbles, crescendos
          again. Of course the wind
    soughs there. Of course
    bamboo moan, chaste, empty

        at heart, where no other plants
    grow, dying in blossom & chanting
        what a human voice
    can't. Insubstantial,
it brings to spring's strophes

        the west wind's antistrophes. Yet
    that's surely the least this garden makes
        as it intones beyond melody
    its old contrapunto,
    its fugue through the years.

THE GARDEN OF SEX

This earth is seeded
        with salt. It blooms

wholly, beatified
        by a thing borne in dust,

undeniable, tender. Its stark rain
        still intimates. It soothes & insists

it never will stop. Why,
        yes, this ground trembles,

relentless. This wild garden grips
        the stem of the brain.

It yields the soft blood's opaque, wet,
        spent fruits. It looks out

past the skin's windowed
        leaves. At the downpour's eye,

warm, this suspiring terrain
        simply swells. Rhizomes reach,

eager, curiously calm. What holds them
        is no more

than surrender that knows
        it too will be fed.

GARDEN AFTER WINTER'S FIRST STORM

Over snowfall, a layer of sleet:
rustling like white leaves, it fell through
night. Borders vanished. The world

is suspended, its riotous differences
almost erased. Here is
what's left. Twigs reaching,

in clear bark that may snap them.
Flat hulls that hang. Wasted pedicels.
Winter's first garden shows

x-rays. These harmonious outlines
are phenomena standing, noiseless,
in self-silhouette, given

dimension by time. Day's moods
in their light become no more
than petals. Out in the sunbed, a dry

rainbow unbolts—buff, umber, cinnamon,
hazel, auburn, sepia, rust. A front
has moved past. The visible

spectrum shifts.

ANGER GARDEN

Listen!
It opposes all efforts. Weeds
      its own shroud. Here, evening primroses

rampage. Bugloss springs coarse-
      tongued, too free. Ladybells prosper, tough.

      Tigertail chokes. Rude cranesbill
smothers. Mugwort's glib fingers

           spread wires. These plants
won't stop. Can't.

      Some work perversely: come dusk,
the aroma of rage intrudes
          unrefused, like belladonna's

      provocative kin, nicotiana.
When you walk, helpless & drained
          as tonight's moon

& difficult, burning, drawn unwilled
      to this sprawl, the crowds cry

      hunger. Jostle. They steal. What
can they offer? Emblems? Astringent

      medicinal leaves?
          Better: narcosis
of perishing. An indifferent

      welcome. A welcome indifference
      in their monotone *now*.

THE GARDEN OF LANGUAGES

You can't draw a plan for it,
can't trace on graph paper how

it lays itself out. In the soil you find
peat, dung, worm-castings, shards

of earth's mantle. You learn bees'
idiom, how they dance locations:

where foxglove, where bergamot.
You know butterflies' semaphore graces it

as birds' war-cries brush past,
& their love-slang. Know it's been uttered

in all the month's dialects: from clear leafy-full
to the planter's subterranean dark.

You can excavate, translate—though
poorly. Can decode a few glyphs

& their grammar. But must know this argot
isn't yours.

(GENERATIONS)

The Garden of Naming

As you pace in its hedge-maze, turning
right, now turning left, you begin
to find prospects.
You might wonder who left it,

cut bog-turf, turned up
that loam. The first
gardener, the man made
from earth? Or the woman who sang

procreation's damp lyrics, gestured
its urgent libretto, till lip
met with lip? Then—banishment?
No profit in those thoughts. Dig

into its doubleness. Accept, blind,
this inheritance: *rain
lilies, blazing stars, mistflowers, switch-grass,
rattlesnake master*... Ponder the verbs

(push, molder, uncoil), their cognates,
their pungent conjugations. Think how
all enact at each temperature
future, present, & past.

FLOWERING JUDASES

In spring, they are manifold, self-sown

or planted: dispassionate pea-flower nubs,
plum-red buds like no human
blood. Rain-mercury branches

spindle toward heavenly brilliance,
a fiction refused them by dense pines,
towering sycamores crowding

creek's bank, north-facing road-cuts.
By the wages of sin against something
or someone said to be other than nature.

As if that could be. Their twigs
are called *spicewood.* Their inner skin
stains. The buds taste sharp, display soft

as peach-blow, as blossoms of apples
in songs about love or this season of kisses,
sacrifice, suppers with bitter herbs,

the palpable's small deaths. Its births.
Season of wrong-headed lusts
for transcendence. Then are earth's

woods a parable? Or a koan, twigs' tang,
the gold dye? And the crucial dear
friend, poor idealist—did he know

that oceans away, five-nerved hearts
would hang down & deciduous trees
would blush, boughs made weak

by his cast-off, lean, unseeded weight?

HAWTHORNE'S EDENS

*My voice swelled and heaved, as if I were tossed up and down
on the ocean, as it subsided after a storm.*
   *—Nathaniel to Sophia, on a public recitation
from* The Scarlet Letter

She piled up fruit, made blossomy
paintings. From his timorous thicket, proud,
he searched his Edens out. His first

came in childhood, all dappled grass, wild
by a Maine lake. To his last (beyond
orchards, the hollow's banks halcyon

with violets)—to that pinery needled
by melancholia's odor, they carried him,
not yet sixty, & old, his restlessness lost

to a locked tower room. But before,
off among rye fields & abundant
raspberry canes, the syringa fluting fleet joys

over the glacial pull of water to lake,
words fountained. Till hedges choked in
again. Earlier still, the best one:

a blithe closure cordoned by willows
& river. A not quite material, belief-
haunted house where *Pond Lily* moored

among cardinal lobelias. Henry
dug rows for their wedding gift: potatoes,
squash, peas. She danced by the music box,

& for a season he left
his autochthonous grief. She lifted
her diamond to cut in the window glass how

the smallest twig leans clear against sky,
inscribing their presence & happiness
(still in their thirties then) *on the gold light.*

The One at Seven Gables

Not his true garden, this. Not the scheme

of his time. A colony-Salem revived
in boxwoods & boxed beds.

He might acknowledge this rough
toothed lovage, this curative gray

santolina. The trellises' iron
antique austerity, too. But he never

did live here. On the trail of bleakness,
he'd visit this steep house. Would speak

of times past among bric-a-brac lavish
as plunder. Drank *camellia japonica*

leaves infused with romance
rooted in bound lives & ancestors' lies:

Let her hang. Dined on Canton plates,
his future's willows & pines laid down

in fancy's dear blue. The kitchen door
horse chestnut (old, verdant, young

while he was, brought in by spoiled money)
rotted out. Now its replica conjures the years

when, unspeaking & writing, writing,
he plowed the maritime streets at night,

husbanding misery & tales, himself
allegorical, his own wicked judge,

bringing dark forward into the caustic
sun of old guilt—& to history's anchorless

censures, a well-tended shame.

The Grass Withereth, the Flower Fadeth

No talent, only genius.
　　—George Sand on Harriet Beecher Stowe

Proved by the light of nature, how soul
might find from grief's Gethsemanes
some small salvation in *a pleasant haunt*
like this one, nursery to withering
memories of dead or shattered children. To
those gardens of the air. Christ's dogwood
here blooms pink, & Tom's petunias,

& others from that cabin's patch:
four-o'clocks, resistant marigolds.
Late in life, her taste ran to Victorian ovals
filled with spiky castor bean. Rain forest
exotics. Beardy plumes. Magnolias painted
(as she wrote, to pay expenses)
& real. In this cottage: sang *Love*

Divine. Her voice cracked, as her brain
did. In her mourning: fern case left
to thirst, the compost heap enriched
by loss. Her green trust? That all would see
her splinter-truths. Her faith? In faithless
dreams of florid groves. Her virtues?
Why—vision, trust, & faith. Such thorns

had got her through the weary tillage
of sewing, childbirths, keeping
house in winter's damp, the kitchen garden one
more chore. Magazine work by lamplight.
On her face, furrows. And her passion,
which became a riven nation's? Only
to cultivate on earth a fairer place.

THE GARDEN OF AGE

Fearful, with little to fear. Dust-purple
asters, the monkshood's last
campanile, orange suns of bittersweet,

snapdragons sheltered, Chinese lanterns:
it makes cunning posies. It might keep
a corner where malachite arrows

of *arum italicum* rise. Nearby,
fresh hellebores, foamflower's tough leaves,
coral-bells, wintergreen heaths: all

intend to hold over. Snow-struck, ragged,
they will. But such a collection
is only a stay. Around it, brittle stems snap.

Pods split like hearts. Seeds submit
to weather's flail, cling to fur, to jeans.
New generations promise. Still,

windfall pears soften. Wasps
drink to their doom. Fear, though—
is it worthy? Does its cause lie

not in ripeness, or damage,
but purely in failure to break?
Well, these are the choices. Crisp, vivid

vases, or a few shoots that spring
in October. The remaining
fruits' satiation. Or delusory whispers.

At the Homestead

Skeleton leaves, so pretty but...not strong enough to publish.
—Thomas Wentworth Higginson on the poems of
Emily Dickinson

Note these gifts—acidic soil
made sweet with terror's
wooden ash, knowledge
that we're *Orchard sprung,*
scents from *Isles of spice.*

Refused, a heliotrope compulsion—
Turned, this matchless earth—
Texts taken up, she hardened off
botany of belief,

made her circuit, tended forms
beyond the stepping stones,
pressed—where paper blots
cold juice—her precise herbarium.

For conservatory's wild delight,
learnt radicle & plume.
In hopes of incorruption,
wove her dry bouquets.

Called home, the zinnias, quinces,
cranesbills, star of Bethlehem.
The same narcissi, doubled,
white—not
skeletal—rise here now.

Her Father's Gardens

Twenty gardens lost and each (he said) a prayer.
Might the next have something for the daughter's
useful arts? Back at Fruitlands, Bronson taught ideal

& immanent, orphic over his New Eden's
aspiring cauliflowers, & transcendental oats
sown cold. All harvested by the hungry girls,

the commune's boy, by constant Abigail—
while the grown men talked. But taught her also love,
or anyway, devotion. And: mind's worth.

He scattered failures. Scattered fine shrubs
at this orchard house. She swore she'd reap
what family needed. *Revolutionary*

elms stood sentinel to moods that gave her time.
Gone, with his viny summerhouse. Today's
tree-bench is a reproduction. As Walden Woods

were mere parterre (a roomy woodlot hemmed
by railroad, fields) where little women studied fishing,
fox-grapes, meadowsweet. Father cried out

the human cost of cotton, cried dream-plots, sugar
maples, paints. Daughter learned intensive culture
of the spirit. Her scribbling gave to sister May

the Tuileries. Bought the mother's final roof.
Her tales bore gardens: Meg's heliotrope,
Beth's larkspur, Amy's bower, & bursting

sunflowers, Jo's, that fed a hen & chicks.
May's brush made callas on this bedroom wall.
So let Louisa's workspace with its view

of cider apples, *Plato's plane tree*, have
within its borders still these painted waxy arums
from their uprooted, bounteous childhood.

Have on the mantelpiece Athena's
prudent bird. And on the spinster's half-moon
desk (he built it), her fruitful inkpot owl.

Ardent Things

I plant the thorn and kiss the rose,
But they will grow when I am dead.
                    —Anne Spencer "Any Wife to Any Husband"

To build a garden is to build
a life. A moonlit work that lives

when noisy days have ended. As this arbored,
weathered, well-pieced *Edankraal* remains.

Here, husband-friend-constructor found her always
reading, making notes that maybe made

her truest poem. Now brittle scraps.
Now ash. Martin came here, Langston, Thurgood,

to sit in day's cool by the lower-garden pond
where DuBois' gift, bronze Igbo head, keeps gazing

at flawless nymphea. Sterling, Georgia,
Marian. Mencken. Robeson. And Jim,

that bold ex-coloured man, releaser of her soul
for whom she wrote *amid these green*

and wordless patterns. Then stood for justice.
For herself she chose *Aloha, Crimson Glory.*

Mothersday. American Pillar. Blaze.
Her plantings, this weedy summer, burgeon,

thick with thorns. She too so long
an *American Beauty* (rootstock Seminole, plantation

owner, this overcast Virginia, various
Africas) goes on. She too, again & still, within

her leafy half-world & a free far country's
eden-home, with words, in words, aflame.

(THAT GREEN EXPIRING CLOSE)

THE GARDEN OF SEX II

Here, purples of salvia cast
tiered whorls of shade

from each dark torch.
Their lingering pungency

masks every doubt.
Their healing denies

any violence, incisions of loss.
They gainsay with blurred

coaxing silences
the sulfurous tansy, its risk,

erasing its
posed oppositions—sly poison

or piquant, sun-stricken herb?
One more thing doubled.

You might wish for clarity. Still,
believe this: there's no wounding here,

no griefs, no deprivation. Only
what seeps & tangles,

denying you nothing, or nothing
you want.

GARDEN OF DESTRUCTION

Peonies shatter. By the blunt end
of summer, trilobate leaves go to rust.

A stick-net of relics
stands. Is cut back. Next spring's red fists

thrust up, if mulch hasn't buried them.
But what they clutch:

their leprous crude drying. The fall.
Do you think a peony clump is dumb hope?

Do you dare to step into one,
brushing profligate blossoms

of satin crepe? You must understand:
neglected, tended, these species flourish

for decades. Must understand: yearly,
they fade. As you will. Will you lay

yourself down on dirt built
of blown petals, skeletal leaves?

The peonies' lips can tell you. Enfold you.
You'll walk into this plot, squared

on its page. Why, then, not embrace?

GARDEN OF RHAPSODIES

Consider, for instance, the *false* or *wild*
            indigo, how
        it holds back,
laggard in spring. Then it happens.

            Through a bare circle
                    of earth, fibrous spikes
                            tear, more
            blue-gray than green.

        Distracted by May's
                voluptuous show (ravishing
                        hyacinths, windflowers' glories,
            &—quick—the loose
                    poppies) you almost miss
            this rush of narrow
                        stalks unfolding.

They sprawl the way violins wing on an improv:

        irregular, certain, tied to melody's lines, & catchingly
                        free. Don't
            think their ecstasy's fragile.

        Under disheveled switches,
                    roots mass, to all droughts
                impervious. When at last
                                the year falls
                        from its heights,
pods hang, drying rawhide. They persist
                            in the cold, not easy
                    to germinate,
            harder to kill.

A Garden Without Chlorophyll

is no garden at all.
Yet such things live,

smooth ghost-flowers shining, fireless
candles in coves

in the woods: coralroot, beechdrops.
Indian pipes. Dull yellow, pinkish, red-tinged,

tawny, or white. Lavender, even, the scaly-
leaved cancer-root. In warm stands

of pine, scarce rosy pigmies
set loose their strong smell of violets.

All colors but one.
These untamable species

are saprophytes, symbionts, parasites,
feasting on rot or what's stolen, or strangely

in intimate partnership. They open
uncanny slick companies

of bells. Dependent. Naked.
Erect. Making gardens

unordered, these, your inhuman
& deviant kin.

THE STILL LIFE AS GARDEN

Pick out the objects

strewn over the table's plane, shaded
by the first gardener's hand,

only after the second, dry tiller of paper,
bestows form & tonality.

Then you may gather their fragrance
from nosegays of markings,

this bright bed in its frame.
Arrived, take your pleasure

in rings of stamens, in leaves' twists,
in authentic dimensions

rendered here just as sun's light
made from seed-points the depths

of ruffled rosettes. No need
to evade. Or hesitate. You have

the right; you are third
in these green generations

of makers, receivers. In your eye,
it blooms, actual: this garden, your own.

THE GARDEN OF MEMORY

A thing done. Recall
how spiked irises

return & return to the iced pond of mind.

How lotuses floating, roots
below frost line in sunken pots, rise

like lost thought
from their anchorage, changed.

See what plants bloom there each year—

if you have the courage. Or in truth,
if you don't. But go back

to the irises: how their turbulent

flags, their stippled
membranous falls,

are stilled in reflection, or shattered

by ripples.

GARDEN OF THE FUTURE

You expect it will come to you, out

of some patient doorway: heaps of bouquets,
wrapped like a lover's pledge.

So you plant bulbs.
On your knees in slant light, you can turn up

soil. Can see how spring rains
will drain, see star-fields of snowdrops,

frilled crown imperials, tulips like lilies,
Anatolian, ruffled. Can see crocuses' pollen,

scilla's blue suns. But
the dangers! You know decay waits

past that door. For voles,
you can bury bulb-cages, or coffin

in gravel the fleshy dried buds.
For the rest, you can hope.

Now you draw in a scent: what
may not wrench out of dormancy.

Yet you know, too, this garden
of them all is most beautiful.

You expect it will come.

The Garden of Memory II

The day of a shadfly
that shimmers, heat's waves

over the pond: these too transit.
In this garden, dry bodies'

paroxysms move with the meter
of months. Here, seasons

extend—species, species,
successions of blossoms come round,

swearing eternity. Don't
be fooled. Each absence,

each subsequent present, each
re-creation has its own architect,

hasty, extravagant, pondering.
The post-baroque resonance

of flies' larval dance
as pond's surface reworks

never repeats.
Will, next time, be spare.

An Aeolian Garden

It is in a mean place & cannot be fine until trees &
flowers give it a character of its own.
        —Ralph Waldo Emerson to his brother William

South of the house, beyond the tulips,
quinces, kitchen rows, the willful
scratching chickens; hard by the pickerel weed
& coppery, echoing mill brook's run, away

from planted hemlocks' shade, alongside
peaches, damask plums: the apparition
& rank incense of the pears. In Concord
seven generations of Emersons, & this

prized fruit in the rigorous new England
still not easily grown. His flourish: Bartlett,
Seckel, Bloodgood, St. Ghislaine, Iron.
The orchardist's duty? To report

their accessible beatitude. So one day
when they wear the color of all colors,
he frees the wind-harp from
its casement, positions it, ruler of airs,

among spring branches, & so lets loose
the metamorphosis of acres resonant
with bees. His memory slips a moment then.
It loses track of how wind can hum

only in a seed-core's sunburst, in grainy
flesh & juice. In blight-puckered habitations
of a sweating slug. Slips, & after
it's played out again in him,

the season's cat-gut insight—how
things are breezily distinguished
& constructed, how they're branch-borne
in that green expiring close.

39

A Garden Imperishable

One of my high ideals...is to remain indestructible
in a perishable world.
                    —Samuel Langhorne Clemens

does not exist. Although he tried, loving
magnificence, scoffing, gilding
an age, making
this house: ebullient gables, turrets, groves
of chimneys, porches with thistle-seed
fret-cut into wood. The Park
River crooked round the hill then, swampy,

fertile, its vistas its own. Under the grid-work
of variegated slates: walls printed
with bindweed & pine needles. Furniture,
floral. Lampshades bearing poppies,
fuchsias, petunias, grapes. Paintings
of hollyhocks. Nasturtiums in bowls,
roses on porcelain, ferns cut

into pewter, vines over brass work, cloisonné
asters. In the nursery, under a bell jar,
strawflowers & lichens. All this saved
not one passing design for money or grandeur.
Nor the daughters, who in solarium's jungle
enacted his books while the river ran,
not yet channeled, murmuring

artifice, artifice, by this full-blown house,
where his best-loved, Susy, flourished
& perished. He pinned his pains-
taking research to his writing room's plain
red walls, its ceiling adorned with dogwood's
faux petals. Plaster. In the worlds he fashioned,
he demanded real things.

.

In Virginia

Whose is the flesh our feet have moved upon?
—Hart Crane

Untouched *jardin anglais.* Or so they saw it,
the opulent sound & tidewater,
this vine-strung woods, *such people
in't,* heaping mounds

for beans, gourds, pumpkins, for increase
of *pagatowr,* yellow, iron-red, marvelous

azure. All *with small labour* husbanded:
thickets simply burned off
amid live oaks & persimmons.
And no man's corn-lot robb'd.

In such a way were the improvident
gold-greedy strangers fed. Was this then
th'unspoiled first metonym for *heaven?*

Was this land to be articulated *Eve,*
this bestower of intoxicating
smoky *uppowoc*—delight to unintelligible gods,
herb that offered rare & excellent virtues

for England's excellent, virtuous *Adams?*
Surely there's another way of reading
open handed, *brown lap'd Pocahontas.*

Another way with hoe or pen
to set out ranks of seeds within a glassless cloche

within the tangled self-sufficiency of berries,
toothsome cattails, chestnuts.
Another way to figure wildness, plant

& live beside that healing *blackdrink*
(yaupon holly, purgative, ecstatic,
ever-green) as the assaulted, lost, blest,
present land awhile *(misnam'd)* endures.

(ANNIHILATING ALL THAT'S MADE)

PARADISE GARDEN

What grew there before
its arrangement?
We know this—within it,

one apple tree blooms
beside an oasis where flowers rise radiant

from water, cradling morning
thrones. Or maybe it offers
ripe fruit & pods that float up,
holding savory seeds.

So. We don't even know:
April or autumn?

Could it have both,
bees burrowing while
on some simultaneous branch
the tart red globes hang?

Impossible! Apples
round & they drop.
Or else sheathed buds
unfold in that cloister.
Dream tells us

this much:
in the Persian enclosure,
those forfeited pleasure grounds,
that serene lotus basin,

in the groomed
bride of earth—in the garden
of paradise, if

time there is mastered,
as it must be, then some

moment from all
must be chosen. Is it
this one?   This?

Gardens of Refuge

Not repose, but abandoning.

Leave, & you'll long
to return. It's possible. Walking the spine

of a mountain, for instance, you step
into a coarse bower of blueberries.

Or find among lichens,
lilies secluded by shadblow.

These gardens too are designed,

in their way. They are, if you'll look,
nearly everywhere: at pasture's edge,

volunteer hollyhocks. Daffodils clumped
in the interstate median once

a dooryard. The butterfly bushes—native
to China—that nod by trailheads

west of the Blue Ridge. All exist
where you see them.

You need only give

yourself over, to enter.
You're safe where nothing's held back.

There where nothing
real pulls you away.

SCAR GARDEN

Held back by cold, this spring's late.
Compressed between weathers

like flesh between flat
glassy plates for the x-ray, they speed:
cherry & crab-tree at once. Ghost-breaths

of pistils hold as small leaves move
forward into their world.

The Bradford's dull symmetry, limbs struck
by windstorm, ice, stands porous
in a new irregular beauty

& pain. Try to see

with the artist's eye how
last year's dry nest sits rough in the fork

& shows you *sleek bark*. See pollarded
trees' knots. See the hills' lesion
where among charred stumps,

houses arise like perennials.
See sinuous veins of freeway, its overpass,

cut through a valley once
roses & groves. As she sees it: the copious
shading, lithe lines

of those forms. And here, now,

her quarry. A keloid
on earth's chest—& alive.
Liquid blue.

Heart's Own Garden

has agile red rooms,
limber canals. It yields

bracts too tender for constancy.
Nonetheless, grown there,

amassed: broken
layer, broken layer.

Each fluid squeeze is a new
bud, each dilation

full blown. Rancid weeds
spring up. Or huge efflorescences

tinted by chemistry. Ill-made
burnt leaves. Gangly trunks.

Seepage taints it. The waterways'
blockage may shut off

its spaciousness. Or some-
times, schooled, its primulas shed

their foliage, rages, their wanting. And so
release all, regardless

of what architect set it
beneath the lungs' plenteous

cloudbanks, adrift
over its landscape of calcium, heavy-soiled

field of what goes.

ALPINE GARDENLANDS

You flew hours, burned tree-ferns
& bird-bones to get here. Yet
they're not it, the gentians' blue, deeper
than summer condensed. Nor the film
of alpen-rose, campion, unforgettable borages,
dwarfed by arête, headwall, cleaver,

crest: not those time-pressed swards,
a whole spring in weeks. Yes,
bristling mid-slope, spruces restore
a scoured forest. In meadows, new
hues mark subtle waterways.
These too fall short.

Pasture & talus, stained brilliant,
can no more than mark, as the eskers do,
seed-plots long gone. But the garden
you came for—cirques, keen seracs,
glassy crevasses—gives ground. You
know why. Fierce dazzle & lavish

out-pourings (like the planet's own cultigens,
the primal pleasance) are being plowed
under, ice rivers turned gravel
by your greed & waste heat. What's greater
is going. Only a sheer white crumpled tongue
could have said *Pax. An end to the ravaging.*

Hurricane Gardens

till the face of the oceans, plow wild
into land. They are certainty, frenzy.

Like any garden, they know themselves stopless—

like scant swings of plantings on barrier islands
where salt-marsh, bight, spit,

cede to a hard cultivator. Erratic,
assured, these gardens sow ruin.

Or escape, when they release
rooftops as if turning soil. Sprung west

of the Azores, rainbands lift. Whorls
batter rough through trade winds.

Pacific typhoons creep grimly past
ilha formosa, then furrow an inland sea.

Across blue earth, corollas coil
around eyewalls. Around absence.

But make no mistake—these gardens
bear fruit. Like you,

they beat their own paths. And will dissipate. Look:

high cirrus petals sweep wide.

Look: altocumulus stamens

red on the radar screen. Look: these skies

trembling. Violent wings.

Mandala Garden

Agreed: divinity's
residence. But it grows

measured, this round
bed of grains tapped

(broken herbs, stone dust, calyxes' crumbs,
powdered seeds—a careful debris)

from the monks' funnels. Exhalations
steady, they tend it, arms propped,

pressed, free. This one's nearly finished.
The gifts on the altar: winged

white tulips. Asters, freesias.
Galactic chrysanthemums,

indigo, yellow, red, gold.
Two weeks since its plot was blessed

with chants like shovels
in suffering's wet clay.

Today, the heartless, poised,
kind gardeners bend low. On the rim,

they inscribe black vines, a harsh
calligraphic fence. It means nothing

that soon amid prayers, these concentric
fields' harvest will be swept up

& poured. Not
quickened. Not dead.

Will slide into river,
a polychrome rainfall.

COMPASSION'S GARDEN

Of course it exists. Let it be grasses, hollow

identical plumes that rise
structural, bowing, the color of manna,
a whole level pampas

light-sown. Each parallel nerve
embraces its own shade.

Each from node to tip breathes

out at night, ease. Winters,
when dense air holds smoke & no

branches move, other gardens
go bare: petioles crumple, racemes fall.
This one stays unmoved.

It does not harbor views. Its foul weed
is pity. It refuses
duality. Frost

is a sword to it. Burned, it springs back.

GARDEN OF SAND

Like all gardens, it shifts.
Like all gardens, no two

share one shape.
The small climates, minerals, moisture,

& light heap up uniquely.
It may ripple in rows, the rake's,

the dunes'. It may adopt colors,
describe a god's palace, scatter

like poppies' scarlet pink orange. Like
poppies, it desiccates

& returns. Its secret is water,
its twin. Its lover's the hourglass rush

out of dormancy. It holds

in its depths blind
tubers, holds faithful

only to rain. Like all gardens,

it's empty. Like all, it's full.

(PLEASANCE)

Each April a Garden

In this one, great lilacs sway.
Rosemary shivers electric in low-pressure winds
moved in after hard rain.

Who can say this garden's name?

Last week was sun-warm.
Bloodroot shone
on the ridge road's swales.
This grey week half the yards in the valley
hold improbable pinks—hasty azaleas,
the last tattered tulips.

Or say what they mean,
wisteria's sham, rock walls draped with moss phlox.
Fool's work

to guess. Home, in pines' shade,
bleeding-hearts hang, the twinflowers
done, wake-robins nodding
above their three lobes.

Sun shifts. Secretive tongues
of hostas uncurl. Ginger widens,
revealing purple-brown cups in the duff.

Snakeweed's blue rubies claim
what they can. This annual host
breaks silence: flesh

is new grass, grass is light's dust, dust
will be wet again, thrown into life.

A Trespasser's Garden

is the possession of no man
or woman, whatever it holds.

To get there, you travel upstream
by unbounded ways, where angelica's airy

unfenced white umbels spring up.
Leave propagation, plan,

thoughts of risk. Move
into the land your presence unfurls.

If you must, you can gather
what's fruitless. Maybe heartsease.

Be circumspect. Seize
the pungent, elusive. No

more. Those cardinal spires, the slender
green dragon, nourishing

arrowhead, rare moccasin flowers,
their lower lips fused:

let them remain. On the unclaimed
threshold of evening, take up

one wordless trumpet, its filaments
full out here, as nowhere. This garden

is not seduced or seducer,
lives only in openings—

of itself, of you.

A Garden Without Mirth

(at Edith Wharton's "The Mount")

This garden has rooms: a house

made of desires turned
under. Her late-blooming
eros, his madness, the other
man's faithlessness—all

denied in frail transformations,
burials. Wildflowers feed
on leaves dropped. In her small
villa, fecund artfulness lies.

Shutters close over walls
to balance true windows; false
windows within, no more
than mirrors. A domain of exclusion

where one woman turned
to severity. Cut away excess to harvest
attention. Framed doors
that won't open. Allowed garlands

in one chamber: its fire-back
shows a dark angel staying
from sacrifice Abram's iron hand.
Black roses curl around it. *Staying*

or pressing? she might have wondered.
Would she have ruin, or illusion?
Heart's seasons? *Ekstasis?*
The fragrance of license

abjured, she chose concealments,
composition's strict rule.
In her bedroom, wrote weak wills'
tragedies, watched snowfall

icing over the hollyhocks' brown.
Built sentences, learned how to grow
realms, her own history
written in wintry cornices, in a suite

painted milk-green, an illimitable sea.

GARDEN OF BITTERNESS

Its soil is not acid, but alkaline—balm
        for lavender's gray plaints.

For prickliness & dismissive, parched
        aromas. Here, in profusion,

baby's breath grows, lover
        of chalks that clog mouth & heart

but open the clay. Here delphiniums
        flourish: glamorous tall

liars who promise glory,
        then topple or mildew,

burning up in summer's true heat.
        Here, spindly clematis splays.

Flirts as it splashes. Succumbs then
        to injury & rot. Scrape

this base mud from your boots.
        Spit on its neediness. Survey it

& laugh. You can replant.
        Use stakes. Use cages, ties,

whatever it takes. Gather armloads
        of weeds. Refill its bland vacancies.

Refurbish. Touch its dirt, sweet
        on your tongue-tip. Don't relent.

In a Walled Garden, as Fall Begins

Giardino segreto: close-laid fieldstone slabs
hold in this unclouded afternoon

& shade. Roofless, taller than head height,

graced by exhausted hydrangeas' globes.
By mottled Italianate creepers, burnt red.

By spent froth of clematis, curved ferns'
heavy leather stems. All this hidden
division. A symmetrical dying.

Better to look to the lawns: sun-laced ranks
of boxwoods mark each terrace,

ascending toward white balustrades.

Or gaze through gray arches.
The pergola's grapevines frame rough-cut vistas:
hayfields, an arm of raw lake.

Geese rest & scatter, scatter & call.
Better to turn back to where each

exact arbor vitae maintains summer's
allegiance. The hostas' lilies have folded.
Maples' leaves, scorched or gold,

have taken the ground. Among them the pool,
where path bisects path, harbors

its rockpile, irregular, perfectly

centered. On it, water can plash down
variant routes. Can be bounded. Made
separate. Keeping its selves to itself,

can merge as it falls.

A Garden Indoors

Someone gathered a great mix
of flowers, set them

safe in this vase,
the verdant, the brittle

utterly loosed
from branches & roots,

defying pesticides, rakes,
clipped & so—

freed: an enclosure

of withering, exempted
from hope.

GARDEN OF CONSUMATION

Where does it rise up? When
does it manage perfection?

Not when seeds of wine-colored basil
breed gems on its tassles, ready

to sow themselves through every bed.
Not when brassy dahlias rupture, late bursts

braying *the equinox nears, let things come*
to balance—the scarlet, the drab.

Not when the whole porcelain theater
of winter unlocks its doors.

To enter this place, strip away

what guards you. Put down your shears,
twine, the trowel that grubs out

weeds. Let sun & rain carry
you (backward,

forward) into raw spring.
Crouch where snowmelt softens,

where east wind crumbles
the clamorous dirt.

You might learn from first shoots,
obdurate saxifrage, the basil's cheap

amethysts, continual saffron-
touched mayapples. You won't root but

you might drink what sky offers,
consuming, consumed.

Why We Make Gardens

Because we need chambers for chaos.
And rows, each like a pilgrimage, strip

mall, potting table, hand-hewn
contemplative bench. Because green-

houses seduce us. Because we are dust
of the planet & hunger

for at least one star's bread. Because we lay
parking lots over arbutus. Because nothing

atones but we like all this digging
of subsoil & root for next year's original

spring. Because plowshares destroy,
& cold frames sweat forth

a fresh crush of thyme, or onions' despair—
all the pathos we find

we invest in such passionless
weeds. Because we fools want

fallacy's wisdom. Because gardens play
dumb. Because they breathe water & make

flames of air. Because we are physical.
Because gardens are not.

(Notes on the Poems)

Hawthorne's Edens

The epigraph quotes a letter Nathaniel Hawthorne wrote his wife, Sophia Peabody Hawthorne, describing a public recitation from *The Scarlet Letter*. Henry Thoreau did indeed plant a garden at the couple's first home, The Old Manse, in Concord, Mass.

During a few months' burst of creative energy, *The House of Seven Gables* was written in a cottage surrounded by fields, in the Berkshires. Other sites mentioned here include The Wayside with its tower writing room and Sleepy Hollow Cemetery, both in Concord.

The One at Seven Gables

The many-gabled house in Salem, Massachusetts where Hawthorne regularly visited his cousin Susan Ingersoll was built in 1668 by sea captain John Turner.

The Grass Withereth, the Flower Fadeth

The epigraph is 19th century French novelist George Sand's expression of her admiration for Harriet Beecher Stowe and *Uncle Tom's Cabin*. Stowe's final home and garden are preserved in Hartford, Connecticut; the words quoted in the poem are hers.

At the Homestead

A progressive thinker and man of letters, Thomas Wentworth Higginson is perhaps best known for his relationship with Emily Dickinson; his support for her poetry was affected by the limited understanding this epigraph suggests.

Her Father's Gardens

The four daughters of philosopher Amos Bronson Alcott and social activist Abigail May Alcott included Louisa and May ("Jo" and "Amy" in Louisa's *Little Women*). Orchard House still stands on Lexington Road in Concord, Massachusetts—some 25 miles from the short-lived commune, Fruitlands, about which Louisa wrote a satirical memoir, *Transcendental Wild Oats*.